The Ultimate Do It Yourself Crafting Workshop

Workshop

4 in 1 Box Set:

Learn How to Master Polymer Clay, Paper Mache, Mason Jar Gifts and Candle Making!

4 in 1 Master

Class BOX SET

Book # 1

Polymer Clay

The Ultimate Beginners Guide to Creating Animals in 30 Minutes or Less!

Table of Contents

Introduction

First and foremost I want to thank you for downloading the book, *"Polymer Clay: The Ultimate Beginners Guide to Creating Animals in 30 Minutes or Less!"*

In this book you will learn how to create your own polymer clay animals. You are going to learn everything you need to know before you ever begin working with polymer clay, including what you need to know in order to choose the correct clay for you. You will learn what tools you will, need and then you will learn how to create cute polymer clay animals.

You will be taught step- by- step how to create each animal, and at the end of the book you will be given tips to help you work with polymer clay. When you have finished with this book you are going to be able to create your own projects and make all different types of polymer clay creations.

Thanks again for downloading this book, I hope you enjoy it!

Chapter 1

Getting Started With Polymer Clay

You have probably seen some amazing creations from polymer clay, and now you're excited to get started making your own creations. The first thing you should know is that you do not need to run off to the craft store and pick up a ton of supplies, which is good news. There are a ton of little supplies you can purchase and most of them cost very little, but if you go out and purchase a bunch of things you will not need, the cost will add up quickly.

In this chapter we are going to go over what you will need, starting with how you will choose your polymer clay. Many different things need to be considered when you are choosing which brand of polymer clay to purchase. One is what the clay contains. Some clay may contain ingredients that you are allergic to, and that is something you need to check before you purchase any clay.

Next you will need to consider color. Color differs with each brand. When you first start out using polymer clay you may work with a few different brands. It is best if you make a small color chip out of each color you purchase, and label the color chip before you cure it. Meaning you will put the brand of the clay on the chip and the color or number of the color for future reference.

By doing this you will be able to learn which colors change on you after they have been cured. For example, some reds may become almost black once they have been cured. If you use this color on a project that you want a bright red on you will be disappointed, but by using color chips you will know exactly what the results will be each time.

Make sure you make your chips the same size and thickness. Consistency does matter when it comes to how your clay will turn out. It is not reliable to use one chip that is 1mm thick and compare it to how a chip that is a .5 inch ball. These are not comparable.

The next thing you need to consider is the structure of your clay. Some brands are going to be much softer than others which mean it is very easy to work with, but since clay gets softer in the oven before it hardens you will need to prop up any parts of your animal that may bend or fall over; such as a horn or leg.

Other clays are harder to work with but hold up well in the oven so you have to decide what your preference is. And there are also clays that are so soft you have to let them sit out in the air for a little while so they become a little harder before using them. This will allow your clay to become the right consistency to work with.

You also want to consider if you are going to be building a base with the clay and covering it with different clay. For most of the projects I do that are larger, I use aluminum foil to create a base and cover it with clay. Some people like to create a base with one type clay and cover it with another. If you are going to create your base with clay you will want to purchase something cheap, like a kid's polymer clay and cover it with a more expensive one.

With all of this information how are you supposed to choose which polymer clay is right for you? The best advice I can give you is to go out and purchase a few different brands and play with them a little bit, then choose which one you like working with the best. If you have hand problems you will probably want to go for softer clay, but if you prefer harder clay you will know which brand to purchase.

The next thing you will need is a working surface. You cannot just use your kitchen table for this. There are two reasons, one: polymer clay is known to stain any porous surface and should not be used in areas where you prepare food. Second: polymer clay will pick up even the tiniest crumb or hair you miss when cleaning, and it will ruin your project.

Instead you should go purchase a simple white ceramic tile. This can be purchased for about 50 cents, and you can create your project and bake it on the tile.

You will need some acrylic paint, roller, paint brushes, toothpicks, glue, spoons and knives. If you need other items for specific projects you can pick them up along the way. Make sure if you use anything out of your kitchen you keep it separate and don't use it for food preparation later.

A few other items you will need is: razor blades, not the kind you shave with but the actual blade inside the razor, an x-acto knife, as well as something to smooth your clay with. You need something more than your finger because this leaves finger prints. A small spoon will do when you are just starting out though.

You can make a ton of different projects out of polymer clay but for the remainder of this book we are going to focus completely on how to make different animals. Some of these will be life-like, and some will be creative, but all of the colors are simply a suggestion. You can use whatever colors you prefer.

Chapter 2

Polymer Cat

The first thing we are going to learn is how to sculpt a simple polymer cat. This cat will be about the size of a quarter when we are finished. Of course if you want to make your cat bigger just start off with a larger ball of clay, but most of the polymer clay projects will remain small like this one.

Start off with a ball of black clay. Using your hands shape the ball into the body. It is best if you can look at a picture of the animal while you are shaping the body out of the clay if you really want to make it look realistic.

Once you have the body shaped, you will want to take four small balls of clay and roll them out to legs. Attach the legs to the body and smooth out the joints. If you want to make your cat sitting down simply make paws for the back legs and for the front, bend the legs in any shape you want.

After you have the legs smoothly attached to the body, you are going to bend a small portion at the bottom to create the paws. You can use your toothpick to make the details in the paws.

While you are working on your cat, you really want to focus on building up the muscles if you are trying to make the cat look real. On the other hand, if you just want a cute little cartoon inspired cat you don't have to worry about the muscle structure as much.

After you have your legs and paws created exactly how you want them you will roll out a small ball and create the tail. Makes sure you smooth out the seam where the tail connects to the cat's body and bend the tail to your liking.

Roll out another ball to create the cats face, and attach another smaller ball where the nose should be. You will smooth this ball until you get the correct shape for the cat's nose. Using the tip of a glue bottle you can create the indents for the cat's eyes. Of course you can use any tool you want for this.

There are tools that are made for using with polymer clay that have a ball on the end, some of them are larger than others but the smaller ones are great for creating indentions for eyes and the larger ones are great for smoothing out clay and creating muscle tone. Now grab your toothpick once again and create the nose holes for the cat as well as the cat's mouth. If you want to add some thin black wire for whiskers you can use your tooth pick to create very small, thin holes or you can use the wire. Do not add the wire now just create the holes. After the cat is baked you will put a bit of glue on the end of the wire and place it in the hole.

Next you will need to cut out two triangles for the ears. Attach these to the cat's head and smooth out the seams. Take two small balls of white clay and create the eyes with a bit of green and black clay as well. You can place these in the eye sockets now, but I find that they usually fall out when baking, instead place them on your tile and let them bake separately using glue to add them to the cat's face later.

Now your cat is ready to bake. Another way of creating a cat and making easier to pose is to create a structure for the cat out of wire. You will create a loop where the head will be, and create a structure for the cat's body, tail and legs. If you want to use less clay you can build onto this structure with aluminum foil and then place small pieces of clay on top of the foil. Smooth it out as you go, but make sure the structure is in the position you want your cat to be in before you cover it with foil.

If you want to add fur to your polymer clay cat after it has baked you will purchase a bit of mole fur or faux fur. Using a paint brush you will add a little bit of glue to each area of the cat gluing the ends of the fur to the cat. This takes a little bit of time since you can only do small areas at a time, and you have to make sure that the ends of the fur attach to the cat.

Once you have covered the entire cat with fur or the areas you want you will need to give you your cat a haircut trimming the fur back to a length that looks natural for the cat.

<u>Watch This Cool Video on Making A Halloween Polymer Clay Cat!</u>

Chapter 3

Polymer Clay Koi Fish

Koi fish are so cute, and they are so much fun to make out of polymer clay. One great thing about this project is that you can simply stick an eye pin through the fish before you bake it and create cute charms or necklaces.

You will need white polymer clay, translucent polymer clay, black polymer clay, red polymer clay and orange polymer clay. Or whatever colors you want your fish to be. You will also need some type of rolling pen; if you do not have a rolling pen made for using with polymer clay a simple marker will do the job.

If you want to make it a charm you will need eye pens, and if you want to glaze the fish you will need some glaze for polymer clay.

The first step in making this polymer clay koi fish is to create the body of the fish. All you need to do is take your white polymer clay or whatever color polymer clay you want your fish to be and create a tear drop shape out of it.

Once you have the tear drop shape you will want to take the smallest part of the tear drop and slightly curve it. Of course this is optional, but it gives the illusion of the fish swimming in the water.

The second step is to create patterns on your koi fish. You will want to set the body of your koi fish to the side, take your rolling pin and roll out the first color of clay you want to add to your koi fish, this could be the red, orange or black (or the color you have chosen).

You are going to roll this out very thin. It will end up being about as thin as tracing paper when you are done with it.

If you have ever seen a koi fish, you will notice that the patterns are not shaped in any specific way. In order to get this effect you are going to tear the polymer clay instead of cutting patterns out. You want to make sure it has a bit of a jagged, uncut looking edge.

Just tear off small pieces of the polymer clay and place it on your fish wherever you want it. You will repeat this with all of the colors that you want your koi fish to have on it. You will want to make sure that you do not cover the entire fish but leave some space in the front where the face will be.

The next step is creating the fins and the tail. In order to create the tail, you want to roll out your translucent polymer clay to the thickness you would like, place your fish on the clay and mark the width of the back of the fish on the translucent polymer clay with a toothpick. This will simply give you a starting point for your tail. After you do this, you need to take your knife and cut out the shape of the tail you want.

Some people prefer their koi to have long flowing tails, while others simply cut out a small cute tail. Connect the tail to the body smoothing out any seams and add any details you would like. You may also like to add a few different colors to the tail like you did to the fish's body. It is completely up to you. Bend the tail in the shape that you want it, and it is time to cut out the fins.

You will once again roll out your translucent polymer clay, and cut small triangle fins out. Then place them to the side of the fish. Another way to do this is to use tiny balls of polymer clay, flatten them out and use one half of the circle for each fin.

Using your knife, you will add the lines on the fins just like you did on the tail. Now you can add the final fin, the Dorset fin on top. Simply roll out your clay, and cut your clay out to the shape you want. You will want to add any lines to this fin before you attach it. After you have added the lines, simply attach it to the top of the fish.

You can also use glue to attach these, but I have found that it is unnecessary and actually makes things harder. You want to make sure the top fin curves with the shape of the fish.

Next you want to take two tiny balls of black clay and create the eyes. Simply flatten these onto the face of the fish. If you want to create a charm, now is the time to add a pin. Bake the fish according to the directions on the pack of your polymer clay.

Once the fish has finished baking you will add your glaze if you choose to do so. Let the glaze dry, and your fish is complete. You can also create mini koi fish ponds out of these fish to sit up in your house. Add them to necklaces, bracelets and earrings to create cute jewelry.

Click Here to Watch This Tutorial on Making a Clay Koi Fish

Chapter 4

Polymer Clay Sheep

In this chapter we are going to learn how to create a simple polymer clay sheep. All you are going to need is white polymer clay and black polymer clay.

First roll out a thin line of white polymer clay and cut it the width of two fingers. You will want to create a lot of these small strips and twist them up into curls for your sheep. Do this by simply taking one end of the strip and curling the rest of the strip around it.

Now you will create an oval shaped body for the sheep out of white polymer clay and attach these curls to the body creating its wool. If you want to save your polymer clay, you can use some foil to create the base for the body and cover the foil with clay. You will find that by doing this you are using less than half of the clay you would have, had you created the entire body out of it.

While you are adding the curls over the body you want to leave one end not covered so that you can add the sheep's head. Don't worry about leaving an area that is too large, you can always add more curls later.

If you want to create a short haired sheep, you need to roll out some white clay into a long thin line like you did for the last sheep. Instead of cutting it in sections of two finger widths, you will want to cut small pellets out of it. Eventually you will end up with a pile of these small pellets.

Take the body of the sheep, whether created entirely out of polymer clay or out of foil covered in clay, and roll it around on the pellets. As they attach, simply flatten them out a little bit attaching them better to the body. Once the body is covered you are ready to move on to the next step with both sheep.

Now you will need to make some flat oval eyes out of white polymer clay. Flatten them after you have made the ovals. Grab your black polymer clay and roll out a snake. You will cut four hooves from this so it needs to be a bit thicker than what you made the wool out of. Roll out a tail, and create the ears for the sheep.

You will also use the black clay to shape the head of the sheep. You will want to create oval shapes that are proportional to the rest of the body. On one end of the oval you will place the ears, and then add the white ovals for the eyes.

Make one hole on each side of the nose of the sheep and use your X-acto knife to create a mouth. Use two tiny circles of black polymer clay and create the pupils for the eyes. Place the head on the body. If you need to add more wool or short hair now is the time that you should do so.

Place the tail on the back of the sheep and the hooves on as well. You can add detail to the hooves, and you will do the exact same thing to both of the sheep.

After you have created both of your sheep you need to bake them according to the directions on the back of your polymer clay. Once they are baked you can add glaze to them or keep them as they are. These are not meant to look like real sheep. They are cute sheep that are more cartoonish than they are real, but they are very cute and a lot of fun to create.

I hope that you have been able to create the projects we have worked on this far. Most of these have been very simple, but the more you work with polymer clay, the easier it will become for you to add more and more details. There will come a time when you won't even need help creating projects.

One of the best tips I can give you: If you want to create realistic looking animals get a picture of the animal to look at while you create it. Using pictures as a reference is a great way to learn.

You will actually want to get several pictures because you will need one from many different angles. You also want to make sure that you get pictures of the same breed of animals. For example if you want to create a beagle, a picture of a poodle is not going to help you create the shape of a beagle. The same goes for different breeds of horses.

One last thing about these sheep, when you are adding the black pieces as the head, tail or hooves, you may find that you are getting black smudges on the white wool, this can be very annoying, but it is very easy to deal with.

One way you can deal with any smudging of colors is by using a polymer clay cleaning technique. You don't have to purchase anything for this. Just get a small cup of water and some q-tips.

Dip the q-tip in the water and rub it on the smudged area. This will remove the smudge. Only use one q-tip per area, and make sure you do not use too much water. Too much water can ruin your entire project. So if the water is dripping off of the q-tip remember it will drip all over your project as well.

This is something that took me a long time to learn and has been a life saver of many of my projects. I will share more tips like this in the final chapter of this book, but for now let's move on to our next project.

<u>Watch This YouTube Tutorial on Creating a Clay Sheep</u>

Chapter 5

Polymer Pig and Turtle

The last two projects we are going to learn are: How to create a cute polymer clay pig and a turtle. For the pig, you will need which ever color of pink clay you want to make your pig.

To begin you will need to roll out a circle of clay for the body, of course you can use foil for this and just use clay to cover the foil if you wish. You will need one circle of clay for the head, two small black circles for the eyes, a small circle of clay for the nose, a small snake of clay for the tail, two small circles of clay for the ears and four small circles of clay for the feet.

You will want to take the piece of clay you have for the body and start to form it into a tear drop shape. Make sure the head is a circle and attach it to the smallest end of the tear drop shape. Take your piece of clay you have for your nose, roll it into a ball and flatten it into an oval shape.

Place this on the pig's face. Next is the ears, you want to roll the clay for the ears into a ball and flatten it into a triangular shape. You want both of the ears to look very similar so you may want to make both before attaching them.

You will not be blending the seams of this pig. You are not working with a lot of detail at this point so you can leave the seams as they are. Attach the ears to the pig and bend the clay creating the ear shape that you want. You can fold it slightly forward to create an ear flap if you want.

Next you will want to put the eyes on, so take your two black balls of clay and place them on the face of the pig just above the nose. Take your tool and make two small holes in the nose of the pig finishing up the detail on the nose.

Roll out your tail to the thickness you want it and curl the tail. Remember that pigs do not have long tails so one and a half small curls is usually enough. Attach this to the back of your pig.

Make each of your balls of clay for the feet into a small tear drop shape attaching the smallest part of the tear drop to the pig's body. You can use black to do this if you wish since pigs do have hooves, or you can use pink. Again, it is completely up to you. Now your pig is done. If you want to add an eye pin to create a charm you will do it at this point. One thing I like to do is get creative with my pigs is add a splash of mud to them.

Remember when we were adding color to our koi fish? You can add a bit of mud to your pig using the same process. Simply roll out your brown clay until it is about the thickness of tracing paper. Tear off sections creating a jagged edge and lay it on your pig creating slashes of mud.

You can also use black to add patterns to your pigs because if you have ever seen a pig you know that many of them have black patches on their skin. It all depends on how realistic you want your pig to look and how much time you are willing to put into your pigs.

You can create a bunch of them to sit up or add them to jewelry. No matter what you do these are very cute as well as fun and easy to create.

Now let's finish up by creating a polymer turtle. I am going to give you the basic steps to create your turtle. Then you can make your turtle on your own by adding the details that you want to it.

For any turtle, no matter what size you choose to make it, you will need a piece of brown clay for the shell or whatever color you choose, one piece of green clay for the head, four pieces of green clay of equal size for the feet, a small piece of green clay for the tail and two tiny pieces of black clay for the eyes.

Of course these colors are just suggestions, and you should use whatever colors you like the most. You can also use very small pieces of white clay to add a bit of detail to the eyes.

First you will want to shape your shell. You will want the top of the shell to be shaped like a mound and the bottom to be flat. You can add a rim around the shell if you would like, or just leave it as a mound.

Next you will take the piece of clay you have for the head of the turtle and shape it however you would like. You can make it a thin oval or a fatter circle depending on how you want your turtle to look.

Attach this to the shell of the turtle. Take the tail of the turtle and shape it into a tiny candy kiss shape or little tear drop and attach it to the back of the shell. Roll the clay for the legs in between your fingers and flatten both of the ends. Attach this to your turtle.

Now you can add any detail to your turtle's shell that you would like and to any other part of the turtle, for example: His feet. Once you have done this, you will attach the eyes of the turtle. Grab a tooth pick and make two small holes for his nose, and you are ready to bake.

Chapter 6

Tips You Need To Know When Working with Polymer Clay

I want to finish off this book by sharing with you a few tips that you should know when you are working with polymer clay.

1. Hand sanitizer will remove any residue left on your hands from working with polymer clay. You should use this whenever you change the color of clay you are working with so that you are not leaving one color residue on another color and ruining your projects.

2. Never use nail polish when painting polymer clay. It will dissolve you clay. Many people do not know this, and they will try to use clear nail polish as a glaze on their projects only to find out later they have completely ruined their work.

3. You can make soft clay harder by placing it between two sheets of paper and placing a book on top. The paper will draw out the moisture from the clay, but you want to make sure you don't leave it for too long or your clay will crumble.

4. You can soften up hard clay too! Simply add a bit of baby oil to your polymer clay and work it in well to make your hardened clay softer.

5. Many people will tell you that you can decorate your creations with sharpie markers; you can draw on the eyes or add whatever you want after the project has baked, but sharpie marker will just fade when you use it on polymer clay. Over

time your creation will no longer have any eyes or features if you use sharpie marker.

6. If you want to keep your polymer clay in the best condition store it in a simple zip lock bag. These will keep the air from your clay, and the plastic in the bags does not react with the clay causing it to ruin unlike some bags.

7. Don't invest a ton of money when you are first starting out. You may find that you do not really enjoy working with polymer clay, and you don't want to waste money on purchasing items you will never use. Instead purchase a few items, try to make a few creations like the ones you learned in this book and decide if working with polymer clay is right for you.

Creating animals out of polymer clay can be a lot of fun, and it can also become frustrating, which is why I did not focus too much on creating life like animals in this book. When you first start out you want to make creations that are fun for you but cute as well. You don't want to take on a huge project such as a large horse, work hard and end up giving up in the end because you didn't take the time to learn how to make simple projects.

Learn simple projects first and then move on to harder projects with more detail, but make sure that no matter what you are doing, you are having fun while you create your projects.

Check Out The Awesome Video on YouTube That Helped Me Out A Ton When I First Got Started Working With Polymer Clay!

Conclusion

Thank you again for downloading this book!

I hope this book was able to help you to learn how you can start creating polymer clay animals on your own.

The next step upon successful completion of this book is to take on some harder projects or create some of your own. Use your imagination and see what you can create.

Finally, if you enjoyed this book, please take the time to share your thoughts and post a review on Amazon. It'd be greatly appreciated!

Thank you and good luck!

Book # 2

Paper Mache:

The Ultimate Guide to Learning How to Make Paper Mache Sculptures, Animals, Wildlife and More!

Table of Contents

Introduction

First and foremost I want to thank you for downloading the book, "The Ultimate Guide to Learning How to Make Paper Mache Sculptures, Animals, Masks, Wildlife and Much Much More!"
The art of paper mache is a fun and inexpensive activity to carry out with your friends and family, and especially with your children. It is also a great way to express your inner creativity. This type of art allows you to let your imagination run rampant while getting messy with glue and paper.
You do not have to have artistic skill on par with Picasso or Michelangelo to be able to participate in this variant of art. Paper mache is friendly towards those who feel like they don't have an artistic bone in their body. It's not about creating magnificent sculptures that result in people gaping in awe rather it is about having fun and letting your imagination run wild. If your paper mache dog looks more like a cow then so be it. It's your dog-cow hybrid thing that you made with your own two hands and you should be proud of it and not shamefully hide it in the darkest dwellings of your closet.
Thanks again for downloading this book and I hope you enjoy it!

Chapter 1: The Tools of the Trade: Everything you need to know in order to get started.

Before we get into paper mache, it would properly be a good idea to actually know what paper mache actually is about. The word paper mache roughly means chewed paper in French. This is fitting as the substances you work with do occasionally resemble mashed up paper. Paper mache can be summarized as the act of combining paper and paste or flour and using these two basic substances to create unique and cool looking figurines. This type of craft has quite a long history, with its basic mechanisms being used in hundreds of years ago in China in the formation of helmets and with the process eventually spreading to Europe where it was practiced in France and England in the 17-19th centuries in the making of wares. You too can celebrate this historic craft by making your own paper mache figures and products. In the first chapter, we will kick things off by gifting you with the tools of the trade. We will list the necessary equipment that every good paper mache novice should be familiar with and also the two chief methods used during a typical paper mache session.

Paper mache is an inexpensive and simple activity, so you will not have a lengthy list of items you will need to purchase or a whole host of jargon and complicated instructions that you will need to memorize. There are only a few items needed and a couple of pieces of valuable information to be aware of before setting out on your paper mache adventure.

This is the great thing about this type of craft; you don't have to have immense art skill or be a Picasso facsimile or have a whole array of expensive art equipment. You just need a pair of hands, a rich imagination and a few inexpensive and easily obtainable items.

Equipment

This is a list of the equipment you will need in order to paper mache.

- **Paper:**This is usually in the form of newspaper, but you could also use magazine paper, tissue paper or just plain white computer paper. It is basically up to you and your particular preferences. But just be aware that some paper will be hardier than others, for example, tissue paper will be quite hard to use and properly will not form a stable foundation. The paper that you decide upon will need to be ripped up into long strips. This is what you will use to create your paper mache masterpiece.

- **A bowl:** This is what you will use to mix your paste or flour mixture.

- **Glue or flour mixture:** Similar to the paper, what you decide to use as your adhesive substance depends upon you. For the glue mixture, you will need to mix a portion of 2/3 white glue with 1/3 cold water in a clean bowl. This mixture will need to be stirred thoroughly until the consistency is to your preferences. However, it should not be too thick. Others prefer to use the flour method.The flour concoction can be made by placing a cup of flour in a clean bowl. Into this flour, cold water should be carefully and slowly poured until it has reached a consistency that is preferable. If it is too thick add more water and if it is too runny add a few more teaspoons of flour. There should be no lumps in your flour mixture, so make sure to stir quite vigorously. Both of these adhesive methods work well and again it is up to personal preference.

- **Paint and a paintbrush**: Paint will be needed when it is time to decorate your paper mache creation. You don't want a newspaper themed dog or pig, rather you want an eye-catching and captivating pink pig or spotty dog. Paint makes your creation just a little bit more special.

- **An extra paintbrush:** This extra paintbrush will be needed in order to mix the glue or flour mix.

- **A balloon:** An inflated balloon is often used for the foundation—what the paper is glued upon to create the paper mache figure. Once the structure has been made, the balloon is simply popped. Other foundation items can also be used, such as a specific cardboard shape.

- **Your creativity:** This is properly the most vital piece of equipment needed for this project and thankfully you don't have to go too far to find it----you already have it lying in wait internally. The process of creating a paper mache sculpture is not supposed to be a chore nor a mechanical process where you methodically put pieces of paper onto the surface of a balloon with a somber expression on your face. This is supposed to be enjoyable. So remember to have fun while doing this and use your imagination when creating your pieces.

The methods

There are two chief methods that can be used when paper mache, firstly the paper/glue method and secondary, the pulp method.

Paper/glue: The paper and glue method is what is traditionally used for the bulk of the paper mache process. This is what creates the broad foundations of your creations using glue and strips of newspaper which are stuck on a balloon or other base item.

Paper mâché is quite an easy activity to carry out. Detailed below is the complete paper mâché process, from start to finish. This will hopefully make the whole process easier.

1. Make your glue or flour paste. Set this aside for the moment.

2. Next, tear up newspaper into long strips. There should be a decent amount of newspaper used as you will properly require a bit.

3. When you have your two main components sorted out, the paste and the newspaper, you can begin to paper mâché.

4. Dip a strip of newspaper into the paste and stick in onto your foundation. Complete the process until every bit of the surface is covered. You should aim to do several layers of paper mâché so that it is stable and not flimsy. After each layer, allow time for it to dry. If you wish for a blank and clear surface to paint over, you should make the final layer with white computer paper.

Pulp Method: The pulp method is used for the more delicate and intricate aspects of your sculpture. So when you have a section that needs a gentler touch, the pulp method would properly be favored over the glue/paper technique. This method involves making a pulp that is then spread over the paper mache form. Below we have listed a series of instructions on how to make this pulp:

Tear newspaper up into small pieces. These pieces shouldn't be too large or minuscule in size. They should be around 2-3 cm in length and width.

1. Place these pieces of newspaper into a bowl and pour hot water over them. All the newspaper should be covered with water. Leave to soak for a couple of hours or overnight if possible.
2. Once it has finished soaking, get your fingers into this mixture. Play around with it---squeezing, stirring and mushing it until it resembles a soggy mush of paper. There should be no lumps. If there is add more water to the mix and stir until it is lump free.
3. Add a pinch of salt. This is to make sure that it does not glob together. And then mix once more.
4. Next grab handfuls of this squashy mix and squeeze out any excess water over the sink. Return the drier pulp back to the bowl.
5. Lastly, add a few tablespoons of white glue to this mix and stir. A pulp has now been created which you can use while you paper mache. This mix can be stored for a few days in the fridge in an airtight container.

For both of these methods, it is important that you lay newspaper out on your working surface. You should also wear old clothes that you don't mind getting messy because paper mache is a messy business!

Chapter 2: Learn how to create paper mache animals

This world is packed with lovely and charming animal friends. Some are scaly while others are fluffy; some are great while others are miniature and lastly some are adorable while others are downright unusual looking. The animal kingdom is a diverse and wild place but more than likely you properly have a favorite animal. Paper mache is a great way to celebrate your love of animals, pay homage to your favorite species of animal as well as crafting a cute little friend for your home.

In this chapter, we have presented simple and easy to follow instructions on how to make four different types of animals using the paper mache method.

A bouncy paper mache bunny

A paper mache bunny rabbit is really easy to make as well as being extremely cute. This would be a great project to do with your children around Easter or whenever you feel like making a cutesy bunny.

So go hop to it!

The equipment

- One balloon
- Quite a bit of newspaper. This should be torn into long strips ready to be used in your paper mache activities.
- Glue or flour mixture

- Some plain cardboard. This should not be too stiff or too flimsy.
- 1 cup of sand
- A funnel
- Paint
- Paintbrushes
- Decorations to adorn your bunny with. This can include googly eyes, pipe cleaners, cotton balls or pompoms and glitter.
- Felt tips
- Scissors
- Tape

The instructions

1. Blow up your balloon. Paper mache* over this foundation with at least 3-4 separate layers. Leave to dry after each layer.
2. Wait until this has hardened and then pop the balloon at the bottom. Cut a small hole into the bottom of the structure. This hole should not be too large, just big enough for a funnel to fit into.
3. Place a funnel so that it leads inside the paper mache balloon shaped structure. Pour 1 cup of sand into it using this funnel and the remove it. Place the foundation upside down so the sand does not escape.
4. Using the cardboard cutout some decorations for your little bunny. This should include some ears, large thumping feet and paws.

5. Using the tape, attach these parts in their respective places. Your bunny now should be looking less like a paper balloon and more like an actual bunny rabbit.

6. We will know paper mache over the messy areas, so the hole you used for the funnel and the spots where tape is visible. Allow this to harden once more.

7. Once there is no more wet paper-glue, it is time to make your bunny pretty. Using the paint, decorate your bunny with any color that you wish. You could have a traditional white or black bunny or a wild pink or blue bunny. It is completely up to you. After you have finished painting, allow the paint to dry. Once dry, draw black lines onto the paws.

8. Now it's time for the last of the decorations. Using glue, paste on the eyes, whiskers [use the pipe cleaners] and a nose and tail [using the pompoms].

9. And there you have it, a bunny rabbit.

Let's chill and make a penguin

Who doesn't love penguins? They are definitely one of the cuter members of the animal kingdom with their little wings and clumsy waddling walk.

Well, now you can make your very own little charming arctic friend, using the following instructions.

The equipment:

- A whole lot of torn up newspaper
- Paste
- A balloon

- Paint
- Cardboard
- Googly eyes
- A permanent marker
- Scissors
- Glue
- Glitter

The instructions:

1. Prepare your paste and newspaper. Blow up your balloon and then paper mâché over it. You should do around 2-3 layers. Leave this to dry, preferably overnight. You can pop the balloon once the paper mâché has dried or you can leave it to deflate naturally.

2. Using cardboard, cut out feet, wing,s and a beak. Paint the beak yellow or orange and then attach these to the body of your penguin, using tape. Paper mâché over this tape and the hole left by the balloon and then allow this to again dry.

3. Once everything is dry, it's time to start decorating. Paint your penguin any color you wish, stay with black and white if you wish for a traditional looking penguin. Otherwise, go crazy with any color that takes your fancy.

4. Allow the paint to dry. Once it is dry, glue on the eyes, define the feet and wings using the marker and your happy little penguin should be complete.

Old McDonald had a pig

Pigs definitely have the cute factor, with their wriggly tail, adorable snout, and bright pink skin. So why wouldn't you want to create your very own precious miniature pig made out of paper and paste. It will be a charming feature to add to your home or gift to a person who really loves pigs.

The equipment:

- Paste
- Torn up newspaper
- Cardboard
- A balloon
- Paint
- Googly eyes
- A pink pipe cleaner
- Tape
- A permanent marker
- Glue
- Scissors
- A paintbrush

The instructions:

1. Prepare the paste and newspaper.

2. Blow up your balloon until it is of a size that resembles a round pig body.

3. Paper mâché over this balloon. Do around 2-3 layers and then leave to dry. Remember to also leave it to dry between each layer. You should leave it for at least 6-7 hours though overnight is best. Once dry, pop the balloon.

4. Using the cardboard, cut out the ears of your pig. For the trotters, cut toilet rolls in half. When your pig is dry, attach these cardboard features using tape. Then paper mâché over the tape areas.

5. Now that you have your pig in a proper pig shape, it is time to decorate. Paint your pig any color you wish. If you want a traditional looking pig, paint it pink. If you want a wild and odd pig, paint it green or purple.

6. Once the paint is dry, draw on the snout using a marker.

7. Glue on its eyes and poke the pipe cleaner into the back of the pig. Twist this until it resembles a curly pig tail.

Mr. Yellow Fluff ball aka a baby chicken

Baby animals are always a fan favorite. There is just something about a cutesy cuddly baby critter that appeals to the senses, you just want to grab them and snuggle them to pieces. Baby chicks defiantly fit this bill being tiny balls of yellow fluff. Here we will show you how to make your very own paper mâché baby chick. This would be a great decoration for Easter or just to have around the house and confuse your poor cat.

The equipment:

- Paste
- Newspaper
- Permanent marker
- A balloon
- Paint
- Googly eyes
- Feathers

- Cardboard
- Scissors
- Glue

The instructions:

1. Prepare your paste and newspaper. Blow up your balloon and paper mâché over it. Leave this to dry, preferably overnight. When it is dry, you can pop the balloon if you wish or let it deflate naturally.

2. Cut out the chick's feet and beak using the cardboard. To make a beak, just cut out a triangle and bend it slightly and then paint it orange. For the feet just cut out triangles. Attach these to the body of your chick and then paper mâché over the tap. Your little chick is slowly forming.

3. Paint your chicken any color you wish. If you want your traditional little chick, you can paint it yellow. Make sure to paint the feet as well. Draw lines onto the feet, adding definition.

4. Glue on the eyes and some feathers to the top of its head, to make some cute little head fluff. And there you have to, a cute fluffy headed baby chick.

We have shown you how to make three cute animal paper mâché figures. But the animal kingdom is a vast and immense arena with vast multitudes of different animals to admire and chose to emulate with paper and glue. Most animals can be made with just a balloon, paint, cardboard and a few decorative aspects. Just spend some time experimenting and discovering your own animal creations.

Chapter 3: How to make bug paper mache models

Bugs seem to get a bad rap. High pitched screaming and expressions of horror seem to be the norm when a spider or centipede is spotted in the home. Noone really wants to cuddle with a sinister looking spider with all those spindly legs and that abundance of eyes. For most people, they just don't appeal to the senses and make you feel that feeling of "aww" you experience when you spot something cute, like a bunny or kitten. However, there are actually a number of different types of cool and beautiful bugs that you can make using the paper mache method. In this chapter, we will present you with all you need to know to create some charming and striking bug creatures, including a bumblebee and a magnificent butterfly.

A Buzzy Bumblebee

Bumblebees are definitely one of the most striking bugs around with its bold yellow and black stripes. Here we will show you how to make your very own eye-catching buzzy bee in only a few easy steps. So get buzzing along!

The equipment:

- A balloon
- Paper
- Paste
- Paint- yellow & black for a traditional look
- Pom-poms
- Pipe cleaners
- Glitter
- Google eyes

- Glitter
- Cardboard
- Glue
- Scissors
- Tape
- Black paper

The instructions:

1. First mix up your paste and tear up your newspaper. Next blow up your balloon and paper mâché over it. You should aim to do at least 2-3 separate layers. Once you have covered the whole balloon, leave it to dry for at least 4-5 hours but preferably overnight.

2. Once dry, pop the balloon if you wish otherwise leave it how it is. Using the cardboard, you should now cut out some wings for your bumblebee. These should be quite large; you don't want your bee to look odd with a big body and tiny wings. Attach these wings to the body using tape. Using the black paper, you should cut out a small narrow triangle. This gives your bee its painful and frightening weapon, the stinger.

3. Paper mâché over the tape areas as well as the hole left over by the balloon.

4. Now it is time to give your bumblebee a splash of color by painting him or her. If you wish to stick with a traditional looking bee, you should use black and yellow paint. With these two paint colors, paint striking stripes onto the body of the bee.

5. Your bee is starting to truly look like a bee. Now there are only a few little minor details to attend to. At present, your buzzy bee is

flying blind so you need to gift it with some eyes. You can do this is in one of two ways, first you can simply glue some googled eyes onto the little fella. Another way to add eyes would be to grab two white pompoms, draw a pupil in the center and then glue them onto the bee. The last thing you need to add is some antennas. You can make these by poking two pipe cleaners through the front of its head. And there you have it, a cute buzzy bee. If you want to make a real special little bee, you could sprinkle glitter onto him or her making for a sparkly eye-catching piece.

A Delicate Ladybug

The ladybug is properly the most elegant and well, ladylike, bug around. There is something very bewitching and appealing about its red and black shell. Having a paper mache version in your home or room will look striking and add a vivid splash of color to your decor.

The equipment:

- A cheap plastic bowl.
- Paper
- Paste
- Paint- Red and Black if you want a traditional looking lady bug.
- Pipe cleaners
- Glitter
- Google eyes
- Glitter
- Cardboard
- Glue
- Scissors

- Tape
- Black paper

The instructions:

1. Prepare your paste mix as well as your newspaper. Get your cheap plastic bowl and paper mâché over the entire thing until there is no plastic left exposed. This includes the underside of the bowl. You have now created the foundation of your ladybug shell. Leave this to dry for at least 6 hours but preferably overnight. When this is dry, tape on six pipe cleaners to the sides, there should be three on each side. These are the legs. Next you need to paper mache over the tape areas and once again leave to dry.

2. When the whole structure is dry, it is time to start beautifying your little bug. First you need to add some color. If you want a traditional lady bug, first paint the whole figure a nice red shade. Leave this to dry. Once this layer has fully dried, it is time to add the quintessential lady bug spots. Using black paint, paint on a number of spots onto the red base. You now have something that actually resembles a lady bug.

3. Now we are onto making the last finishing touches to your bug. So, glue the eyes on and make the antenna using glue and two pipe cleaners. Lastly, if you want a sparkly lady bug you can add some glitter. Use glue to make some patterns on the lady bug, for example a love heart or spiral, and then sprinkle some red or sliver glitter over this. And there you have it, a glittery and striking lady bug.

A Scurrying Spider

The truth of the matter seems to be that spiders are creepy and pretty unlikeable creatures. They lurk in showers and on ceilings, a monstrous horror that causes many to scream and scramble out of its proximity. Spiders are generally quite scary and sometimes the protagonist of your nightmares. For example, watching a spider devour its latest web ensconced victim is just plain disturbing. But a paper mache spider is harmless and can even be considered kind of cute in a creepy kind of way. Furthermore, a paper mache spider would be a great decoration choice for Halloween.

The equipment:

- Paste
- Torn up paper
- Two balloons
- Paint
- Paint brush
- Pipe cleaners
- Goggly eyes
- Red and white paper
- Scissors
- Craft glue

The instructions:

1. Prepare the paste and paper. Blow up one of the balloons to a reasonably large size. Paper mache over it and leave to dry. Take the second balloon and blow it up, but keep it at a small size. It should be the size of an apple or orange. Paper mache over this as well and leave it to dry.

2. Once both paper mache foundations have dried, attach the smaller one to the larger one using glue. Paper mache over the seam so it looks natural. This is your spider's head and body complete.

3. Paint over the structure in any color that you wish, for example a midnight black looks quite dynamic. Once the paint is dry, you can start adding the traditional spider adornments. For the eyes, if you wish for a true spider look then make sure to glue on eight separate eyes. For the legs, attach eight pipe cleaners, four on each side. You can attach these, by poking them into the structure. Now your spider has its many legs and eyes, the last thing you need to do is give it a fang filled mouth.

4. Using the red paper, cut out an oval shape. Next, using the white paper cut out two small triangle shapes. Glue the triangles onto the red paper, and then glue the red paper onto your spider. And there you go, you have a spooky spider.

A Beautiful Butterfly

So we have just instructed you on how to make one of the creepiest creatures out there, now we will show you how to make the beauty queen of the bug world, the butterfly. There is something whimsical and graceful about butterflies. The way they seem to seamlessly glide through the air. The butterfly is the epitome of grace and beauty. Well, with a few simple ingredients you can replicate this beauty and make your very own paper mache butterfly. You should defiantly opt to hang this butterfly from the ceiling in a representation of flight, as any true butterfly should be presented in.

The equipment:

- Paste
- Torn up newspaper
- A long cardboard tube
- Scissors
- Glitter
- Paint
- Paintbrush
- Glue
- Pipe cleaners
- Cardboard of any color. This will make your butterfly's wings so chose a color that you find pretty or appealing.
- Paint brush
- Jewels and other decorations

The instructions:

1. Prepare the paste and paper. Grab your cardboard tube and stuff it with newspaper. Paper mache over this entire structure, effectively trapping in the newspaper. Leave to dry. This is the body of your butterfly.
2. Using your colored cardboard, cut out the wings of your butterfly. These should be decent sized, not too small or too large. Attach these to the body of your butterfly using tape. Next, tape on two pipe cleaners, these are the antennas. Paper mache over the places where there is tape.
3. Now it is time to start decorating. Paint over the body of the butterfly using any color that you want.

4. Using the glue proceed to make cool patterns on the wings. These could be spirals, hearts or stars. Basically anything that takes your fancy. Sprinkle glitter over the wet glue. You could also add small jewels, which you can find at a craft store. This will make your butterfly's wings very pretty and eye catching.

Chapter 4: It's time to celebrate with paper mache: How to make a mask and piñata

Do you want to stand out at a party? Well, wearing your very own paper mache mask will properly get you noticed. And it makes a good ice breaker, where you can talk about how you made the mask and the inspiration behind it.

Furthermore, homemade piñatas are normally a hit at kid's parties. Including a brightly colored figure filled with candy is sure to go down good with any kid and frankly any adult as well. And it always looks better if you put the effort in and make it yourself.

In this chapter, we have given you the instructions on how to make a basic mask and piñata design. You can modify this to your own preferences as your skill increase with this art form.

A paper mache mask

A paper mâché mask is a great piece of decorative apparel that you or your child can wear at a themed party or a Halloween celebration. With a few simple ingredients, you can create an enchanting and amazing looking mask.

The equipment:

- Newspaper- torn up
- Plain white paper-torn up
- Paste
- A gallon jug with the labels removed.
- Paint
- Paintbrush

- Decoration items, including jewels, feathers, pipe cleaners, glitter, and anything else that you wish.
- Scissors that are capable of cutting through plastic
- Glue
- Paper mache pulp

The instructions:

1. Get a clean gallon jug and cut it in half lengthwise. Take one half and turn it upside down. This will act as the foundation of your mask. Cut out two eye holes, a mouth hole and two holes on either side of the mask.
2. Next, using the newspaper paper mache over the jug until you have done 3 layers. Do not paper mache over the holes. After it has completely dried, paper mache using the plain white paper. Leave to dry completely, this should be preferably overnight.
3. Using paper mache pulp, which we described in the first chapter, make the detailed features of the mask. For example, if you are aiming for an animal mask, make ears and a nose using the pulp. Be creative during this stage.
4. Now it is time to individualize your mask through decoration.
5. The first thing that you need to do is paint the foundation. How you decide to paint it will depend on what you want your mask to look like. If you wish to make a tiger mask, you would paint it orange with black spots. If you wanted a mime mask, you would paint it white. The same goes with the adding of decorations, it is largely up to you. Let your imagination run wild at this stage. If you want to make a bird mask, you could add feathers or for a

beautiful entrancing feminine mask you could use a lot of glitter and mini jewels. Make a mask that resounds with you.

6. Once everything is decorated properly and also dry, string through an elastic string or a ribbon through the two side holes that you made earlier. This will prevent your mask from falling off.

Let's make a piñata

A piñata is always a party favorite, mainly because it involves a shower of candy and chocolate. You can purchase a ready-made one from the store or you could unleash your wild imagination and make your own using the instructions supplied below for a simple round piñata.

The equipment:

- A round balloon
- Paste mix
- Torn up newspaper
- Paint
- A paint brush
- Glitter
- Brightly colored tissue or crepe paper
- Scissors
- Glue
- Tape
- Candy for the filling

The instructions:

1. Prepare your paste and newspaper and set aside.
2. Blow up a round balloon. Paper mache over this foundation. You should aim to do around 2-3 layers.
3. Next, it is time to paint the piñata. Taking into account, that this piñata is properly going to be for a fun vibrant party it is best to paint it a dynamic and luminous color. For example, purples, reds and yellows would be a great choice.
4. After the paint has dried, it is time to make your piñata festive. First, glue on long strips of tissue or crepe paper around the span of the balloon. Carry on doing this until you have covered the entire thing.
5. Next, get more colored tissue paper and cut it until small strips. Each of these strips should be around 2cms across and 3cms lengthwise. Glue these onto your piñata, so that they are facing upwards. Only glue the top half down and leave the bottom half free. This should make a cool ruffle effect.
6. Once you have created this look all around your piñata, it is time to fill it with candy. If the balloon that you used as a foundation is still inflated, you should now pop it. Once the balloon is popped, add the candy thorough the hole made by the balloon. Cover the hole using tape.
7. Finally, tape a ribbon or string onto the end of the piñata. You will use this to string your piñata up.
8. And there you have it, a colorful round shape structure that kids [and adults] will have fun hitting with a stick in a quest for sugar.

Conclusion

So, you have reached the end of this book on the basics of paper mache. I wish to first offer you my thanks in first downloading this book and then taking the time to read it.

I hope this book was able to help you to learn the basics of paper mache as well as how to create some cool paper mache sculptures.

The next step upon successful completion of this book is to go out and practice. Utilize your imagination and own ideas when getting messy with paper and glue. Don't follow rigid instructions but have fun and make your own strange and unique constructions. The thing about paper mache is that it is supposed to be about having fun. So remember to do just that.

On a final note, if you have found delight in this book, I urge you to please take the time to share your thoughts and post a review on Amazon. It would be really welcomed!

So, goodbye, thank you and good luck on your paper mache adventure!

Book # 3

Mason Jar Gifts:

The Ultimate Guide for Making Amazing DIY Mason Jar Gifts

Table of Contents

Introduction

I want to thank you and congratulate you for downloading this book, Mason Jar Gifts: The Gifts the Keep Giving. This book contains proven steps and strategies for enhancing the joy of the holiday or birthday party of your loved one through choice of the perfect gift. In addition, this book provides cheap and easy recommendations which can make this dream come true, personalizing your gift to show the receiver of it just how much you truly care.

If you take the time to read this book fully and apply the information held within this book will help you to understand the many creative possibilities of gift giving Mason jars provide. If your family is anything like mine, you go through jam and jelly pretty fast, and thus probably have some jars just lying in the pantry. Why not put them to good use? Peruse through the information in this book, which was written to entertain as well as educate, and learn just how you can spice up your holidays with a Mason jar gift.

This book continues as follows. It consists of six chapters. The first chapter discusses the many benefits of Mason jar gifting. The second chapter makes recommendations for Mason jar gifts. The third chapter covers how to decide on the perfect thing to put in your Mason jar gift. In the fourth chapter I talk about how these gifts can be made and given depending on the holiday or special occasion. The fifth chapter addresses sharing and celebrating Mason jar gifts with your family. The sixth chapter covers all the great things you can do with your jars if their contents have outlived their usefulness. Finally, the last section concludes.

At the end you'll be an expert on Mason jar gifting, and one of the best gift givers around. They say that it's better to give than to receive. I can't say with full certainty that I'd want to give away such a well-suited present. When I see the look on my partner's or my best friend's face when he sees it however it all becomes worth it. Thanks again for downloading this book, I hope you enjoy it!

Chapter 1

The Many Benefits of Mason Jar Gifts

There are so many benefits of giving Mason jar gifts that it's hard for a writer to know where to begin. This section outlines some of the reasons in the attempt of spreading the joy of the Mason jar gift as a preferable option.

First of all, Mason jar gifts are very practical. They're inexpensive themselves, and often recycled from their use as a container of food or condiments in the house. Yet they carry a strange stylistic effect of being appropriate for gifting despite this high functionality and prior usage. This is essentially the best of both worlds. In these tough economic times, it's really important to have something that is thrifty without compromising the quality of the gift. Mason jars are just such a gift, also because they can be doubly used for practical purposes by the receiver after already serving great purpose to anyone who has owned them in the past.

The second great benefit of this gift type is the versatility of the options for what can go inside it. More ideas are given with respect to this in the second section. But essentially, anything that can fit inside the jar can be given, as well as a nearly unlimited combination of small gifts that can be enjoyed one by one. This also means that the gift can be intensely personalized, and well-catered to the individual. It's considered a great sign of respect and informs the closeness of a relationship when a person can choose the perfect gift, because this often requires a lot of knowledge about what he or she is interested in. Lots of small gifts can be the perfect formula, or rather if the receiver loves all of one thing that much more, maybe that's a sign for the giver to keep things simple.

These days' practical gifts are often preferred to extravagant ones. Also it can be unreasonable to expect someone to reciprocate when given a really expensive gift. Instead, give them something they can use practically around the house and they'll be grateful. One doesn't always need to have diamond encrusted earrings when more practical needs must be met.

While a Mason jar gift can be (very) inexpensive if that is the desire, keep in mind that great things come in small packages as well. Moreover, a Mason jar can be the perfect place to conceal something of great value, like jewelry. The effect of this on the receiver can be even higher, because generally one does not expect to receive a gift of such import in a Mason jar. Engagement rings too might be an excellent option!

If you're interested in more specific options for gifts and the methods used to make them, check out the next chapter, which provides 30 different gift ideas for those that need a push in the right direction. In later chapters I discuss how you might best match up your gift depending on the person.

Chapter 2: Gift Recommendations

This chapter discusses many of the wondrous options for Mason jar gifts. Brief and easy descriptions are provided to make them, whereas some of these can be store-bought. Of course a special sentiment is always expressed when more effort is put into the gift, especially when you decide to go to the trouble of making the contents and decorating the gift yourself. Design and gift ideas vary. Some of them are for practical usage in the household. Others provide aesthetic improvement. Some are simply good to eat. Everyone likes to have delectable food items around. Take a look below to discover new gift ideas in these 30 recommendations.

1. Poured Candles

Either buy a jar with a pre-made candle or heat and pour your own wax. Be sure to leave the wick intact and sticking out. These are available in a variety of aromas that will add to the holiday atmosphere.

2. Candy!

This is the simplest gift ever. Fill the jar with candy that your loved one likes most. The perfect jar decoration for this gift is a soft paper exterior held together with a rubber-band near the cap.

3. Canned Goods

Peaches, apples or pears are always great to have in a canned, especially during the winter-time when they're out of season. You're bound to have cravings. Less than extravagant, this is a practical gift that is appropriate for everyone.

4. Herbs and Spices

Let the jar be a dispenser for your loved one's favorite herbs and spices. This may require a set of jars, perhaps smaller ones. Lots of families make a point of collecting spices over the years. Share with them a special spice that's used in ethnic food that they haven't tried before. This way you can help them expand their horizons as well.

5. Soap Dispenser

Drill a half-inch hold in the lid and screw on a dispenser pump that you can purchase at a local arts and crafts store. Also, these are available to purchase pre-made. Add whatever soap you want and help to save the world by avoiding excessive usage of plastic.

6. Sewing Kit

A key for winter warmth, sowing enthusiasts will love a quaint way to store their materials, and will think of you every time they need to take them out again. This may even make them a bit more likely to sow you your own new set of hat and mittens!

7. Twine Dispenser

How about this for practicality! Put your rolls of twine inside, and all you need is a small hole drilled in the lid. You can even stack them and have various threads coming out, so you'll only need one jar to dispense all of your twines.

8. Salt and Pepper Shaker

Spice up your dinner with salt and pepper shaker jars. These too come pre-made or can be made based on your preferences. Some people are satisfied with ordinary salt and pepper, but the connoisseur may require a subtler taste!

9. Light Display

Drilling holes in the sides of the lid allows you to string up your jars. Putting lights in them creates a special kind of effect, a nice ambiance for the porch. Light up your friends and relatives holidays by giving them a lighted Mason jar gift set.

10.   Bathroom Accessory Holder

Mount those babies on the wall and you can put your toothbrush and other morning implements in them. You might even think ahead of time to fill the jar with a set of special toiletries, one of the most practical gifts ever!

11.   Photo Frame

Put old photos of you with your friends or family in the jar, so they can remember the times that you've had together. The slimness of this gift will leave the rest of the jar open to special surprises, including other little trinkets to celebrate and remember your past.

12.   Speaker

Check this out. You can purchase Mason jars that have been converted into external speakers. This is like a cross between a stereo upgrade and the perfect gift for grandma. Your music will sound better coming from Mason jar speakers.

13.   Liquid Dispenser

Give your family or friends a Mason jar that's got a tap built into it so that they can fill it with whatever liquid their heart desires. This would be a wonderful little alternative to a family pitcher at the dinner table, and certainly adds character to the set.

14.   Cooking Implement Holder

How about filling up an oversized jar with cooking tools? The implements will probably need to be sticking out from the jar, so this present is probably best wrapped and filled in bubble wrap as well to conceal the cooking goodness and to protect the integrity of the glassware as well.

15.   Cookie Dough

If you want to give away a special treat, fill up the jar with a rare and special kind of cookie dough. This gives the receiver the homework of doing a bit of baking, but the aroma and the taste of the cookies will remind your friends of you. Try wrapping the lid up in a little bow that matches the color theme of the evening.

16.   Layered Salad

This one obviously can't be kept under the Christmas tree for any extended length of time, but it allows for a special surprise in the short time. Take it with you to picnics. Salad on the bottom, then carrots, radishes and tomatoes are added, and finally, salad dressing on top. Mix it all up and enjoy yourself in the park.

17.   Past Letters and Correspondence

If there's someone you have a close relationship with, perhaps a spouse or a significant other, and you want to reconnect with them, copy down your past correspondence on nice sheets of paper and include them. Also put in there some blank sheets of paper and a nice pen to give that special person the incentive to continue writing you in the future.

18.   Cupcakes

Bake up a storm with cupcake molds that are shaped like your Mason jar glass. When finished simply be careful in taking them out and putting them in the Mason jar glass. What are the holidays without ample sweets?

19. Birthday Gifts for Kids

Fill up a Mason jar with assorted colorful birthday materials. Balloons, chocolate medallions, paper hats and mini toys are a great way to show that you care. This is the perfect mini birthday kit.

20. Flowers

Go out to your garden or to the flower shop and pick out something that will brighten your spouse's day. Flowers are a classic way to show that you care, and while the flowers themselves will wilt, the jar will remain a useful gift.

21. Coffee

Nothing makes the coffee drinker happier than getting surprise exposure to new kinds of Arabica coffee. Fill the jar with one kind of coffee or an assortment. The receiver of this gift will have to thank you endlessly for helping him or her wake up early in the morning.

22. Tea

Assorted teas can be as great to drink as coffee, especially late at night when one doesn't want to be kept up all night by caffeine. There are all sorts of teas around the world. How about some mint leaves too? It only takes five minutes of soaking to completely change the taste.

23. Hot Chocolate

Had enough drink ideas? If you haven't considered making a gift of hot chocolate it's time to get with the program. This is a perfect gift for when it's cold outside and adds comfort to the winter of even the worst scrooge.

24. Mason Jar Lamp

Get a lamp that can be mounted on the wall or stands alone. These will add character to the bedroom or living room. Best store-bought unless you've got some carpentry skills, these make for the perfect lighting implement.

25. Oil Lamps

Fill a jar up with oil and set the wick atop alight! Many of these jars come with aesthetic contents that make the jar look easier on the eyes. This is a longer lasting alternative to candles, and also is great for the environmentalist as it takes you off the grid.

26. Quick Bread

Include nuts, gingerbread and chocolate chips for a delectable mix of goodness that everyone will enjoy.

27. Glowstick Jar

Empty the contents of a glowstick into your jar, and add diamond glitter to the mix. This is the perfect gift for a young princess. Be cautious in making this as the materials can be harmful

28. Wineglass

Believe it or not, there's a special kind of Mason jar that's a play on wineglasses. These are store-bought, and perfect to pull out when you're looking for a twist in a romantic evening.

29. Pasta

Nothing spells home like pasta with all the herbs and spices included. Far better than a box of noodles, include seashell pasta pieces so they'll fit.

30. Salsa

These jars are perfect if you want to have some salsa and chips in a sports gathering. Create your own concoction rather than relying on the store bought stuff.

Chapter 3: Deciding on the Perfect Gift

If you like the idea of giving a Mason jar gift but are not quite sure in exactly what form to give it to your loved one or co-worker, take a look below for lots of options. Gifts are always more interesting when they're personalized, and different types of people like all sorts of things. Of course, the type of gift you give should also depend heavily on your relationship with the person in question, ranging from the informal to the intimate, and the familial to the professional. Don't worry though; there is an appropriate gift for everyone.

Co-Worker

Gifts in these circles are usually characterized by fun little trinkets or gags that try to mock the over-serious tone that gets taken on in some of our workplaces these days. Quite often, gift exchanges are carried out during the holidays, meaning that you may not need to worry much about the contents of the gift at all, especially if it's going to be selected by a co-worker randomly. We all love having secret Santas. Office-related implements are great, a new stapler, for instance, to replace the one that your co-workers have been wrestling over all year. Just remember though that a workplace gift is a workplace gift. If you want to give something intimate to one of your co-workers, it may best be done in private.

Friend

Depending on how well you know each other, you might be able to go all out with a gift for your friend. You probably know what he's been wanting all this time better than anyone, so go for it if you're feeling particularly generous. Good friends often enjoy throwbacks to when they were kids, electronics, and hobby-related gifts. We all need a pair of socks every now and then, but that's where you grandparents come in. Friends are supposed to buy each other gifts that are exciting.

Parents

Parents are generally happy that you remembered to buy them something, and you should, as a small token of appreciation for all the stuff they've put up with over the years! Your parents may already be worried about accumulating too many random trinkets that they'll have to find a place to put around the house, so think practical when it comes to the parents. Cater to your mother's feminine side by getting her candles. Flowers can also be hugely meaningful. Your father might be glad to get some tools, although not the same ones that he got last year!

Siblings

If your brother or sister has just had children, s/he may want something that can help with the baby. A cute light display would be wonderful. Otherwise, how about something relating to their interests? You are sure to know them about as well as anyone.

Significant Other

Now things are getting intimate. If you're what you would consider a serious couple you may want to step it up with the gifts. These could somehow inform your special relationship. Unplanned gifts can make his or her days unpredictable in a wonderful way. Clearly this is one of the few relationships where it might be appropriate to introduce some spice into things.

Spouse

Now that you're married, you can think of gifts as more practically things that might work well around the house. Be careful in presenting something however as a gift that you both might need. A special kind of food or drink in a jar may do the trick, or another option is to hide that small valuable gift in a Mason jar, making it that much more of a surprise.

Grandmother

Last but not least, don't think that your grandmother won't enjoy a Mason jar gift as well. In fact, she may be able to reminisce about the times when these were how general stores used to stock their goods on the shelves! Now, that is certainly cause for nostalgia. So what is the perfect gift for grandmother. This may be difficult considering that she's accumulated so much stuff over the course of her life. This may be a valuable clue though. Grandmothers often have collections, and are glad to expand them, although in the end it's the thought that counts.

Grandfather

If you can distract your grandmother for long enough, you can justify getting grandpa a jar of whisky without getting him into trouble. Otherwise you may have to choose something more suitable to the tenor of an amiable evening with the family. Grandpa might like some nails for his workshop so he can get out of the house or maybe even a special kind of sweets.

Chapter 4: Seasonal Gifting

When it comes to maintaining relationships, the best way to show that you care is to make a real effort when the holidays roll around, and get creative in your holiday themed gift ideas. Consider the symbolism behind a gift, and remember that giving is always better than receiving. Mason jar gifts allow you to spread the love around cheaply. Way better than getting nothing, get a person in your life a little something. In may not seem like much, but a little goes a long way. That small sentiment could really make someone's day.

Often, having those extra presents around on a birthday just makes the event seem grander. At Christmas, too, you don't want one small gift under the tree, even if it's a great one, what you really want is an overflowing of presents so grand that people can hardly walk in that part of the room. This doesn't require giant expenditures but it does require some forethought. Also remember that there are all sorts of holidays throughout the year. This chapter takes a look at how you can celebrate the holidays with different Mason jar gift ideas.

The first are the most obvious. Holidays like Christmas host times in which jars are gifted, often with a visual theme to match. These express the Christmas spirit faithfully. There's no reason not to give out Mason jars on Hanukah as well. They can be filled with dreidels as well as anything else. Mother's day and Father's day are a great time to show your appreciation to your parents, and let's not forget your grandparents too, even if there isn't a designated day for them. Valentine's Day is a must for lovers, and the perfect time for men and women to say that secret nothing that they've been meaning to utter for months. Wedding anniversaries must always be remembered by husbands, and are a wonderful way for married couples to celebrate the years they've spent together. Shorter term couples may also enjoy their one-month anniversary, though this may only be the beginning of a great relationship!

Saint Patrick's Day is perhaps the most appropriate holiday during which to gift a Mason jar filled with booze. Just make sure you don't give the same person too many or he may get too drunk and fall into the Chicago River by accident! Halloween on the other hand is quite clearly perfect for spookily themed gifts of candy. Dress it up as a ghost and place them around the house afterwards to add to the scary atmosphere or take the empty jug and fill it with spooky lights. There is virtually no end to the themed gifts you can give during the holidays.

You probably wouldn't want to fill a Mason jar with turkey, but on Thanksgiving candy corn is a suitable gift. After all, thanksgiving was all about gift giving, not just stuffing your face until it's completely full! Share that wondrous candy corn! One might not know what to give on a leap year, but it's certainly a rare occasion. Make something up to celebrate this too! Weddings are beautiful occasions, and also a time of gift exchange. The groom could certainly use a couple of cigars to celebrate, and the bride will need a new garter to replace the one she's tossed. On birthdays you've got to take the individual into account, but it should clearly be something that caters to a particular taste. Don't forget what the receiver likes! And remember that above all, it's the thought that counts.

There are other times when people celebrate special events in their lives. High school and university graduation are two big ones. These days computers are a popular gift for high school graduates, but remember, a smart phone may fit within a jar as well. University graduation is an important time too and should be celebrated comparably. After this, a person must go out into the world and transition from being primarily a receiver of Mason jars to a giver of them. This can be a difficult thing to get used to, but with the information here at hand, it should be no problem at all! And how about Bar and Bat Mitzvahs? All the children of the world deserve Mason jar glasses.

Chapter 5: Share and Celebrate!

Our first recommendation in this chapter is to make one of the jars that you give to someone else as a present to someone else as well. Honestly, you would do this for your kids if you had to go out and buy a birthday present for them to give to a friend of theirs. Now it's time to enjoy the spoils of your own generosity. One for them, one for you, that's how the system should work, and this way everybody is happy. Share the joy of these presents with everyone. Holidays aren't the only time to give presents. Sometimes giving presents when they are unexpected is when they are appreciated most.

Celebration is about getting together and sharing your presents as well. The beauty of giving spices away in a Mason jar is that the family will taste them in their food for months to come. It might even become a staple, and fundamentally change their family's recipe. This sort of impact explains why it can be so rewarding to watch the positive impact that you have on people's lives. Mason jars make this a possibility like few other gifts can, especially due to how versatile they can be.

Imagine how fun it would be to sit across the room from one another on the warm and cozy carpeting in your living room with the fireplace ablaze, sharing your gifts with everyone. And afterwards the jars get placed on the mantle above the fireplace for all to see. In a way, they're similar to the surprises in one's stockings. Mason jars are the little wonderful unexpected gift that serves the holidays like an appetizer serves a meal, whetting one's appetite for the real big presents which are to come. Without that little preparation, opening a giant present is too abrupt. Five minutes, and the experience is over. No! This is not how it should be. Unwrapping gifts is meant to be a long and arduous process, at times exhausting. The more gifts you give the more exhausted you are when they are finally opened. But this is a wondrous kind of exhaustion that means you did your best in preparing to take care of your loved ones.

This is a process that nearly all grandparents are familiar with, and they love to shower their children, and mostly their grandchildren with gifts. Grandparents, aunts and uncles have the great gift of being able to spoil their grandkids, nieces and nephews, simply because they aren't around them all that often. Older folks also have the benefit of probably having a lot more Mason jars around than their younger counterparts. Why not take advantage of this?

Chapter 6: Uses for Mason Jar Gifts Afterwards

If you've been given a Mason jar gift and are not 100% sure with what to do with the jar afterwards, here are some ideas. You can get some use out of it around the house in an inventive way. The interesting thing about these jars is that despite their original intention as gifts they seem to look appropriate in just about any of their possible functions, adding a stylistic feel to the house that can be quaint and surprisingly charming. There is a comfort and a pleasure to be found in the many clever ways one can turn an ordinary jar into an appropriate trinket to enrich the cultural and visual atmosphere of your home.

The first and most obvious use for your Mason jar gifts is to hold on to them as a remembrance of the experience of receiving them. Gifts represent the kindness of the gift giver, and his desire to see the receiver express joy in the instance that it's received, and hopefully these positive emotions are maintained throughout the course of any relationship. Sometimes it is easier to connect with that warm feeling of having been cared for through the act of gift giving by having these remembrances around.

Despite how great they might make you feel some people simply don't have the room to collect dozens of empty jars on their mantle. Thankfully, Mason jars are one of the few gifts that it seems are totally appropriate to re-gift. If you've got one too many, don't feel bad about filling them up with some candy (or brandy) and gifting them off to a friend. They'll be grateful for either, and generally will not even be able to tell the difference between this jar and another.

If you'd like to keep the jar but find another use for it, here are some ideas. Mason jars make for great candle holders. Fill them up with water and set alight a floating candle, providing a special romantic ambiance that's even more significant because of your contribution of creativity to the mood of the room. Or, try simply using the jar as a mug for drinks. Some of the classiest venues prefer to use jars for their cocktails. There's a funny kind of irony in this in that jars are used for storing. Since the container is generally bigger than one serving, drinking from a Mason jar sort of feels like tapping liquid straight from the source – it makes your drink look deceptively large, which may be a welcome plus during trying holiday season. Parents will find these especially useful as their glasses will get broken more often, so the replentishing of any kind of glass will be a relief.

Gardeners will find that Mason jars make the perfect tiny little garden patches to put around the house. The glass gives a wonderful cross-section view of the roots, so you can see your plant's progress both above and below ground, making sure that it has plenty of water. Small herbal plants are a great choice for your indoor garden. This keeps them conveniently accessible when you need them for cooking, as well as nearby so that it is more difficult to forget to water them.

If you want to get really inventive, drill a hole in the lid and make your Mason jar into a soap dispenser. It will add so much more character to the room than would an ordinary plastic bottle of branded soap. It also really personalizes your bathroom and makes it your own. It is little trinkets like this that make one feel comfortable at home. This same strategy can also be used to make them in condiment jars. Instead of using cheesy plastic bottles, customize your home dining experience by adding something of your own character to it. For the perpetual snack-eater, a jar is the quintessential holder of all sorts of goodness. Cookies, mints, M&Ms, and skittles are all very much at home in a Mason jar. They keep you stocked up on sugar while you're sitting, reading in your living room, and provide guests with a nice little touch of refreshment with little effort on your part.

Conclusion

Thank you again for downloading this eBook!

I hope this book was able to help you to learn about using Mason jar gifts to show your friends and loved ones how much you care, and that you always know exactly the right gift to give. The next step is to put this information into action and get started in devising your Mason jar gift ideas. The guide above hopefully was of great help in figuring that out.

Just to reiterate, the chapters were as follows. Chapter 1 explained the many different benefits of getting a Mason jar gift. They're cheap, easy, practical and have many uses. Chapter 2 went through a long list of gift ideas and combinations. This should be of help if you're stuck and not exactly sure what to get. Chapter 3 gave a number of specific recommendations for Mason jar gifts, along with a basic guide for how to make or get them. Chapter 4 discussed how to think of the perfect Mason jar gift for the different people in your life. So much variety! Chapter 5 talked about the warm celebrations that you'll enjoy with your family over the years, as well as the joy of both giving and receiving Mason jar gifts. Last but not least, Chapter 6 discussed what you can do with your Mason jar gifts when the presents inside them are all said and done. Plenty of options are available.

This chapter concludes this eBook. Finally, if you enjoyed this book, please take the time to share your thoughts and post a review on Amazon. It'd be greatly appreciated! Thank you, good luck and happy gifting!

Book # 4

Candles

The Ultimate Beginners Guide to Mastering Candle Making

in 60 Minutes or Less

Table of Contents

Introduction

I want to thank you and congratulate you for downloading the book, ***Candles: The Ultimate Beginners Guide to Mastering Candle Making in 60 Minutes or Less.***
This book contains proven steps and strategies for making your own candles in very creative ways, and all in less than sixty minutes. It takes you step by step through a wide variety of materials that you can use to make candles, things that you are able to get very easily and at low or no cost at all. In addition, it shows you how to make different kinds of candles to suit your occasion. From this book, you will be able to make candles that use wax as their main ingredients, and others that do not use wax in the least. This book generally teaches you what to do to put your creativity into practice as far as candle making is concerned.

If you take the time to read this book fully and apply the information held within this book will help you to make your own candles any time you wish, selecting ordinary materials from what you have in your possession, and making very useful candles that are often eye catching and nice smelling too. Above all, each of those candles will only take you a couple of minutes to make; and in some cases, you can make a number of them concurrently. Essentially what that means is that by the time you are through reading this book, you will be in a position to assemble a heap of candles in less than an hour, and all the work of your own hands. How encouraging!

Thanks again for downloading this book, I hope you enjoy it!

Chapter 1

Popular Use of Candles beyond Lighting the Room

You may be among the lot that knows a candle for its utility value. Particularly in remote villages where electricity is unknown, the well-to-do make use of candles as lighting items. Oh – and what, you may wonder, do others in such areas use? Well, many of them use tins with a wick and paraffin.

The emphasis here, however, is on the well-to-do; and this is so as to get a chance to point out that candles are not that cheap if you are planning on buying them off the shelves every time you need them. Therefore – what?

Therefore, there is need for us to be equipped with the basic skills of making a candle. You never know when you might need to make some. You could find yourself in an unlit area where even ready-made candles are not available.

Why else would anyone want a candle?

Others may wish to reverse that question of *why else* and ask: How, for the love of beauty, can one live without candles? How beautiful they are especially when they come in different colors! And that brings us to the other uses of candles.

1) Aesthetic purposes

Evidently, some people love candles for aesthetic reasons. The sight of candle flames in a background of total darkness is very fascinating. Also the not-so-glaring light adds to the ambience of the environment and creates just the right atmosphere.

On this very scope of aesthetics is also the aspect of scent. You can make nice smelling candles all on your own without having to spend too much sourcing from shops.

What candle fragrances exist?

It is fair to say that you can get as many candle fragrances as there exists perfumes. Some of the available fragrances include:

> Citrus Tango and also Frankincense; Apple and Pine Needle; Black Cherry; Garden Sweet Pea; Honey Glow; Lilac Blossoms; Mango Peach Salsa; Pink Grapefruit; Spiced Orange; Vanilla Lime; and Wild Fig.

2) Religious purposes

There are many religious organizations that use candles at their place of worship, and also during various rituals. In the Christian religion, some denominations like the Catholic use candles in church on a daily basis. One purpose is to make their place of worship beautiful. So, here, it is about ambience. The other purpose has religious connotations because the light of the candle represents God's own light. And that is why if a candle goes off during mass, the main ceremony in the Catholic worship, some church attendant moves immediately to re-light it.

Even Buddhists use candles, placing them in their shrines and wherever there is the image of Buddha. These candles are complemented with flowers and even incense. This is a way of showing respect to Buddha. The candle light is representative of the light that Buddha's teachings give.

In Judaism, candles are lit to mark the start and end of the weekly celebration of the Sabbath. The first set of candles is known include the Shabbat candles and they are lit on the evening of Friday. The other set comprises the braided candle, which is one candle bearing several wicks. This one is lit on the evening of Saturday and that is to mark the end of the Sabbath. Of course, it also marks the start of a fresh week.

3) Culture

There are people who are not religious and are not concerned about the beauty of candles, but do value candles for the role they play during cultural rituals. For example, Hebrews light a candle whenever they are observing the death anniversary of a loved one.

4) Magic purposes

Many people have associated candles with magical tricks and rituals over the years. But even for those that do not care much about magic, most still find something mystical about candles. Many are the families that plant candles on a cake and have the Birthday Child make a wish as he or she blows out the candles. That indicates some level of belief in magic.

For the very serious magic oriented, they often wish to make their own candles to ascertain their purity, and also to have a chance to transmit their personal energy into the candles long before use. In fact, the whole magical process involving candles embraces some key connotations. Like the fresh unlit candle representing the earth; the burning of the candle and having wax melting representing water; and the emission of smoke by the candle being representative of ordinary environmental air. And also there are meanings associated with the different colors. That is why you may wish to know how to make your own candles so that you can produce colored candles as you prefer.

What does candle color signify?

When you have a personal reason to use a candle, you do not have much patience to explain your beliefs, but instead you want to get on with it. Let us, nevertheless, explain what the users of colored candles associate with the respective colors:

a White

A white candle is said to elicit peace. It also carries the element of spirituality.

b Red

Red is associated with popular human qualities and strengths particularly sexual potency; energy; strength; and courage. That is why people are known to burn red candles when initiating or hastening the healing process.

c Pink

Pink is linked with the popular and soft attributes of affection; love; and even romance.

d Yellow

Yellow connotes great memory and creative streak. It is also associated with great imagination and intellectual capacity. You will find people burning yellow candles to increase the chances of passing an exam.

e Green

Color green is associated with good luck; harmony; fertility; and even abundance.

f Blue

Blue is said to give you inspiration. It is also associated with protection; devotion; and also magical wisdom.

g Purple

Purple is the color associated with superior psychic ability; great spiritual power; and also idealism. It is also linked to material wealth.

h Orange

This color is associated with great achievements regarding personal ambition; matters of law; and also career.

i Silver

This is a color associated with inspiration; intuition; clairvoyance; and also lunar related energy.

Chapter 2

Existing Varieties of Wax For Candle Making

Can you ever be good at something without knowing the basics? Of course, you cannot. That is the case with candle making. Luckily, there is very little you need to know before you begin to make your own candles. Just as you need the necessary ingredients to make some lovely dish, the same way you need some specific ingredients to make lovely candles. Here are the materials you need to make candles:

1) Candle Wax

Oh, how does this one look like? What amount do I need? Well, we seek to answer that and make you fully equipped with all related information. Ultimately, you will be able to make candles of different kinds to serve different purposes. For starters, you need to know that candle wax is not uniform. There exists different types and they include:

2) Paraffin Wax

This is the one that has been in use for the longest time ever. It actually is still the most commonly used. The paraffin the wax is made from happens to be a by-product of the process of refining the very crude oil from deep down the earth. So in some way, paraffin wax is a by-product of Petroleum.

It is also good to know that this wax in varieties when it comes to melting points. Some melts faster than others.

And how different is paraffin wax from other types of candle wax? Well, it is:

- Fairly cheap
- Easily catches the color
- Easily catches the scent
- Melts faster than others

All the same, you need to realize that some people will find the smell of some chemicals in it somewhat irritating as the candle burns.

3) Soy wax

This one is made from soy beans, and though not as widely used as paraffin wax, it happens to be gaining popularity pretty fast. Of course, it is somewhat more expensive than paraffin wax; yet people find it a popular alternative natural wax that does not smell strong.

In summary, the reasons that contribute to the growing popularity of soy wax include:

- Being relatively slower in burning. What that means is that the soy candle lasts longer than many others. Even then, it is good to know that even the soy wax in varieties with different melting points.
- Being pretty easy to clean the wax off surfaces.
- Having eco-friendly usage and not being irritating to anyone as it burns.
- It is also renewable.

An additional point to note about soy wax is that it easily blends well with beeswax and other ingredients like vegetable oils of the coconut and palm varieties. In fact, there are also soy candles that have a bit of paraffin wax too.

And with this you may wonder, when do we cease calling it soy wax if it is mixed with other ingredients?

Well, it is like a company buying into another one. When it acquires 51% shares in that company, the other company ceases to be mentioned; the one with 51% shares has control – influence. Likewise, as long as the candle wax has 51% or more of soy, then we call it soy wax without trying to hairs.

4) **Soy wax also comes with different melting points for different varieties.**

a) Beeswax

Beeswax is entirely natural and is therefore safe to use. It is also not a new creation; obviously older than soy wax. The earliest beeswax was found in the pyramids of old. Beeswax is actually made by bees in their honey making process. So its natural state is not in doubt. Its lovely scent depends on the flowers from where the bees had gotten nectar, prior to the bees excreting the wax into honeycombs that then house and incubate the larvae.

5) **Beeswax has evidently its unique qualities and those ones include:**

- Having its own pleasant scent
- Combining well with essential oils
- It has ability to purify the air around it as it burns

However, it has shortcomings like:

- Not retaining added scents for long
- Not retaining added color for long

Beeswax is usually packed and sold in slabs or blocks. Sometimes too, it comes in rolled sheets, in which case you would not need to melt the wax; rather, just rolling the sheets into candles.

b) Gel Wax

Gel wax is made of hydrocarbons from mineral oil, and often mixed with resin. A special kind of polymer is used to thicken it into the burnable wax that it is. Gel wax is different from other types of wax in that:

- It has a clear look
- It burns much slower than paraffin and vegetable based kinds of wax.

c) Palm Wax

Palm wax is made from palm oil. That tells you that it is all very natural. But what exactly draws people to it?

- It is eco-friendly and does not emit unfriendly fumes when burnt
- It makes candles that burn for a comparatively long time
- Its candles happen to produce relatively bright flames
- It comes from a source that is renewable so no natural resources are being depleted by making palm wax.
- They are very nice to hold as they are not sticky. On the contrary, they are hard and feel smooth.
- They are strong and so they do not easily bend or even melt

d) Recycled wax

Wax that gathers after candles have burnt out can be melted again and re-used as new candles. Of course there are always the bits of remnants that gather as the candle burns – mainly the melted candle wax – and that is what becomes your main ingredient for your fresh candles.

Chapter 3

Learning the Basics of Candle Making

Would you rather you had one way of doing things or different ways of doing those particular things? Without a doubt, you are better off with a choice. Fortunately, you can have more than one way of making candles, most of which will take you literally minutes! And this is our agenda today: learning to make candles in less than an hour.

We are going to learn some of the greatest but easiest choices of candle making, but we better review the basics first.

What do we need to make candles?

Well, you need to have:

- A melting pot
- Wax
- Fire
- Wick

That is basically all – items that are fairly inexpensive and easy to find. Now let the fun begin.

Generally, this is how it goes:

You light your fire; and you need not worry what kind of fire it is. If you use firewood, the assumption is that you have an idea how to control the heat because there will be a point where you will need to keep that heat under check. Otherwise the other sources of heat like an electric cooker; gas cooker; and such, happen to have their temperature gauges that are pretty easy to use.

So, whatever wax you have chosen – of course not the wax sheets that are ready to use – put it in your melting pot. And do not worry yourself with the type of pot to use as any will do. In fact, if candle making is something you want to do often, you only need to use an ordinary cooking pot once, and that pot will always feel ideal thereafter. So you then put the pot on the fire and begin to heat your candle wax. With this, you will see the wax begin to melt after only a few minutes.

A question that may dog your brain: What happens if the fire is very hot? Well, you will be fine with very hot fire; you just will not let it get too hot. Reason...? Beyond some point, say 212°F, you are in trouble because your wax could easily burst into flames. To be clear, every type of wax has its optimum heating point that you need to target.

Here are some specific candle types and how to make them:

1. Dipped Candle Torches

You can already tell there is some dipping that will take place here; and you, obviously, can only do dipping in some aqueous substance. So how do we go about it?

Let your wax melt in its entirety. It would be great if you were equipped with a thermometer, because then, you would be able to measure how hot your wax is at different stages. The most important of all is the optimal point, which in the case of Dipped candle torches is 160° F – the point at which is recommended you begin to build your candles.

- You get hold of your wick, dip it carefully (yes, carefully – you are dealing with hot stuff!) into the wax.

- Then let that wick rest inside there for a couple of seconds before pulling it out. Do you realize that from an environment of 160°F to room temperature there cannot be any other way for wax but cooling and solidifying?

And sure, that is what happens to your wax that is now well glued to your wick.

- You then do a repeat move: dipping your waxed wick back into the hot wax. As before, you let it lie in there for a couple of seconds, even just two seconds are enough; and then you pull it out and let it cool.
- That is the process that you need to repeat until you have gotten yourself a thick candle.

Believe it or not, the whole process takes just a few minutes. But supposing you wanted your dipped candle torches to have some fragrance or color?

- Well, that is easy. You just add the necessary ingredients, if it is essence or your choice color, add them to the candle wax as it heats. And there – you have yourself some nice smelling wax that is colored as well!

2. Votive Candles

Let us look at what you require before you embark on making motives:

- Appropriate Wax
- Wick
- A Votive Mold (preferably metallic)
- Pot to use in pouring out melted wax
- Thermometer

If you wish to color your candles or give them some scent, then you, obviously, need:

- Your chosen dye
- Your chosen fragrance oil

Votive Candle Making Process:

- Heat your chosen wax to a temperature of between 165°F and 185°F when it is ready to be poured out. Optimally, however, the wax needs to be at 175°F at this juncture.
- It is time to put in your additives in case you have some to add, and mix them well. By additives, we are referring to things like stearic acid, which is a wax hardening substance, or even vybar, a substance that eliminates any bubbles there might be.
- Follow that up with your fragrance oil
- Finally add your dye.

Mind you that sequence is important especially because you need your wax to remain in its original color, so that each time you add something you can monitor how well it is mixing. And you realize that is something you cannot do after you have added your dye to the mix. **You now have your candle wax ready to pour out into the Votive molds.**

- Prepare your molds to receive the wax by coating them thinly with a mold release agent. We are talking of a Silicon spray or something like that. Of course, you realize this substance is not meant for the candle wax; it is just a facilitator. It is meant to make the candle get off your mold with ease.

- Then prepare the surface where you want to place your votive molds by spreading some absorbent paper like an old newspaper. The purpose of such material is to absorb any liquid that accidentally spills as you pour wax into the votive molds.
- Now pour out your melted wax into the votives, maintaining a continuous flow so that you curtail the formation of bubbles.
- Let that wax sit for a few minutes to cool a bit and then insert your wick. Why let the wax cool somewhat?
  - Just like you may fear a little bit to get your fingers burnt, there is need to worry about your wick; excessive heat might adversely affect its firmness.
  - The not-so-hot temperature is fitting for getting the wick's metal tab sticking to the bottom of the mold. And that is important because it then becomes the central hold for your wick.

In fact, if you see like your wick is far from straight and you want to rectify that, you just need a few more minutes for the wax to cool further – and what is happening in the meantime? Well, the wick's metal tab is getting more firmly held onto the mold. So once you are confident that has happened, you can pull at the wick and direct it to the direction you wish just to make it straight.

Some votive wax shrinks on cooling, leaving some space in the middle that calls for you go make a refill. And then – what happens next?

Well, that is so, but when we are talking of making candles within 60min, we have the option of using votive wax that is referred to as 'one-pour'. That way, you will not have to pour in more wax and wait for it to cool and solidify. In fact, the recommendation is that you place your molds in some cold bath of your choice to make the wax cool faster.

How to handle the votives when ready:

Now you have ready votives that are ready to be removed from their molds. Once you are confident they are properly cool, remove them and place them some cool place ready for use. Just in case you find that some votives are still not exactly cool, it is suggested you put them right in your freezer for about 5min; and if you find them not cool enough, you keep them in the freezer a little longer.

Of course, when you want to light your votive you normally will want to place it in a clear glass where everyone can see it properly. And just for information, that votive candle will last longer in a glass, whatever the wax you have used, than when you place it on your chosen glass plate.

3. Container Candles

You can use the same method to make container candles as you used to make votive candles, with only some small variation. The difference is that when you pour wax into your container, you do not remove it afterwards. Once you have inserted the wick and the wax is cooled down, that is the end of it. That is the container you will be lighting the candle from.

Chapter 4

How to Make Candles Without Using Wax

Why are we interested in knowing how to make candles fast? That is
something you may wonder. But guess what? You will not always
have accessible lighting like electricity or lanterns. Besides, there are
times you may have lanterns but run out of fuel. There are other times
you may just want to keep lighting costs down.

In learning how to make candles without the use of wax, you need to
appreciate that you may wish to make candles with wax but miss the
wax itself, which is the main component. For instance, you may go
camping and carry candles to last you for the days you plan to be out
there. But supposing something unexpected happens and you are out
in the woods longer than you envisaged. That is the time you realize
how important it is to have the skills of making candles without wax.
Here you are taking into account that, at the time, you have no place
from where to buy ready-made candles or even wax.

Here are the alternatives nearest home:

Candles made from canned meat

Does this sound outrageous? Maybe – but when you are actually in
dire need, you think in an extraordinary way. In the unfortunate
scenarios mentioned before we got here, mourning or even whining
about running out of candles provides no solution. On the contrary, it
is important to learn how to create your own source of light and fast
at that.

The message here is that any canned meat that has lots of lard inside, or even plenty of vegetable oil, serves well as a candle of sorts. This is how you go about preparing your lighting:

- Pick your wick and measure it against the height of your can. Once you get that height, make your wick double that length. And you are possibly thinking: For goodness' sake, someone better explain to me how I would go camping or a long walk carrying a wick just for the heck of it. Surely, it is quite unlikely, that you will think of wicks as you pack items like bottled drinking water and snacks. But hey! We spoke of thinking out of the box. So here you are going to make your own wick out of the material you have. Do not wonder how to do this. Here is one of many ways of making your own wick in minutes.
  - o **First of all get the items you need ready. In this case we have:**
    - A pair of scissors
    - A piece of cotton string

The going is simple:

- Cut your cotton string to the length you deem sufficient
- If you have some lard or oil around where you are, soak your string right inside. If you do not have some, no worries.

And hurray! You have a canned beef candle.

- Take your nail and make a hole in the centre of your can of beef.
- Push your wick inside the can until you have only about ½mm exposed on the surface of the can.

- Take some dish expansive enough to accommodate your can

Your make-shift candle is ready for lighting at this juncture. Once you light the ½mm length of self-made wick, you can enjoy that light for a number of hours.

Candles from wax crayon pieces

Why throw away broken crayons that are too tiny for drawing work? You can use it to make candles when need arises.

This is how you do it:

- Put your different pieces of crayons in a can – any can, even a soup can.
- Put water in a pot and place the pot on fire.
- Now put your can of crayons inside the pot of hot water and wait for the crayons to heat up and begin melting. You need to wait for your water to begin boiling.
- Once your pieces of crayons are well melted, your final move is to pour the wax you have just created into a mold.
- Now take your wick and insert it in that mold when it has cooled a bit.
- Ensure the wick is well centered by tilting it with your hands even as the mold continues to cool down and solidify.

Candles from candle remnants

Here, you only need to follow the example above where you build candles from remnants of wax crayons. Once your different stubs are well melted, you just insert your wick, either bought straight from a selling store, or a wick that you may have made just from local material available to you.

Candles from Bayberry

Is this not the plant known for its medicinal properties? Well, it is. But a plant can have more than one single use. Consider how waxy Bayberries are. It is not surprising, therefore, that they should come in handy when we need candles and we do not have the usual candle wax. See here below how Bayberries produce candles for you:

- Take a pot or other container and put water.
- In that water put your Bayberries
- Put the container on the fire and let it heat to a boil
- As the boiling takes place, your Bayberries are producing natural wax.
- Now get your container off the fire and let it cool down.
- Get hold of something like a spatula, spoon or whatever else that can help you remove the layer of wax that is, by this time, sitting as top layer on your water.
- Take a piece of candle stub and melt it and then pour that melted wax on your chosen mold. Once it dries up, it will serve as your strong base for your wick.
- At this point, insert your wick.
- After that pick the container with your Bayberry wax and empty the contents into the mold.
- Let that wax to cool down and you have yourself a great candle ready. Note that at this point you are referring to a very nicely scented candle as the Bayberry plant is nice smelling.

Chapter 5

Other Candle Types You Can Make In Minutes

Just to reiterate the value of being creative, you can make your own candles and use them for lighting or decorating your zone in the manner you wish, even when you are short of some of the conventional ingredients that we know like wax and ready-made wicks. At times, you can readily have wax but not the ready-made wicks, and other times you can have ready-made wicks but not the candle wax you are used to. Whatever your predicament, you will benefit if you have the basic skills of candle making, and the guts to put your creativity to test.

Take advantage of the following tips and you will the better for it:

i) Lard Candles

Oh – lard? Yes, lard. You may know it in cookery, but then what ever has one function? You write with your hands and use the same hands to eat. You use avocado as a fruit and still use the same for cosmetic purposes. So, in the spirit of thinking outside the box, here is how you make candles out of lard:

- Take a small empty tin.
- Put some lard in a cooking pot and heat it till it melts.
- Pour the melted lard on top of the tin.
- Take about four strands of, let us say, twine, and then dip all of them into the lard.
- Even then, let about 2.5cm of the twine remain standing out as the lard goes dry.

This is a process that takes you only a couple of minutes and you can now light the tip of the twine, which is now your wick; and there! You have a self-made candle. Have in mind that you could decide to use lard that you would otherwise have discarded, thus making your candle making undertaking a fairly cheap one.

ii) Toothpick Candles

To make these ones, you will need the following simple items:

- Toothpicks
- Candle wick
- A pie pan dish
- You may also add some of these items just to make your candle a bit more attractive and desirable:
  - o Some fragrance
  - o Some dye
  - o Some glitter

Right: what do you do then with these items? Well, here are the simple steps you take to have your candle ready for use:

- Put the wax in a pot and put the pot onto a fire to get the wax melted
- Pour melted wax into your pie dish
- Add your fragrance into the wax
- Then add your dye into the wax too
- Now that the mold is a bit cooled, pull it out of the dish that is serving as your mold
- You can cut that block of wax into regular shapes as you wish just before the wax becomes entirely dry.

- Insert a toothpick in each of your pieces of wax; and do not push the toothpick too deep otherwise you will risk breaking the wax.
- On one end of each piece of wax, attach a wick

The toothpick candles are significantly used to decorate things like cupcakes so you do not need to worry about them burning for long. The main lesson you need to take from these lessons is that you can apply different methods and different ingredients to make candles, even those methods and ingredients that have not been documented. As long as you now know the basics of candle making, and what you will agree is the common sense of keeping your hands free from hot wax, lard and other oils, you can make a wide range of candles any time you wish. Above this, your speed in making candles – minutes and not hours – will make you proud.

Conclusion

Thank you again for downloading this book!

I hope this book was able to help you to appreciate the different methods you can use to make candles wherever you are – home, camping, or traveling. It is also my hope that you now appreciate that it is not mandatory that you have ordinary candle wax in order to be able to make candles. It is also my hope that you understand what you can do when you want to make unique and customized candles, either for a birthday or special dinner, and what to do when you want to accomplish that in an unprecedented short period of time.

The next step is to put the information and skills that you have learnt into practice, and get confident in making your own candles. I also hope that you will be able to practice that knowledge to increase your speed of candle making.

Finally, if you enjoyed this book, please take the time to share your thoughts and post a review on Amazon. It'd be greatly appreciated!

Thank you and good luck!

Bonus Chapter: Seasonal Gifting

When it comes to maintaining relationships, the best way to show that you care is to make a real effort when the holidays roll around, and get creative in your holiday themed gift ideas. Consider the symbolism behind a gift, and remember that giving is always better than receiving. Mason jar gifts allow you to spread the love around cheaply. Way better than getting nothing, get a person in your life a little something. In may not seem like much, but a little goes a long way. That small sentiment could really make someone's day.

Often, having those extra presents around on a birthday just makes the event seem grander. At Christmas, too, you don't want one small gift under the tree, even if it's a great one, what you really want is an overflowing of presents so grand that people can hardly walk in that part of the room. This doesn't require giant expenditures but it does require some forethought. Also remember that there are all sorts of holidays throughout the year. This chapter takes a look at how you can celebrate the holidays with different Mason jar gift ideas.

The first are the most obvious. Holidays like Christmas host times in which jars are gifted, often with a visual theme to match. These express the Christmas spirit faithfully. There's no reason not to give out Mason jars on Hanukah as well. They can be filled with dreidels as well as anything else. Mother's day and Father's day are a great time to show your appreciation to your parents, and let's not forget your grandparents too, even if there isn't a designated day for them. Valentine's Day is a must for lovers, and the perfect time for men and women to say that secret nothing that they've been meaning to utter for months. Wedding anniversaries must always be remembered by husbands, and are a wonderful way for married couples to celebrate the years they've spent together. Shorter term couples may also enjoy their one-month anniversary, though this may only be the beginning of a great relationship!

Saint Patrick's Day is perhaps the most appropriate holiday during which to gift a Mason jar filled with booze. Just make sure you don't give the same person too many or he may get too drunk and fall into the Chicago River by accident! Halloween on the other hand is quite clearly perfect for spookily themed gifts of candy. Dress it up as a ghost and place them around the house afterwards to add to the scary atmosphere or take the empty jug and fill it with spooky lights. There is virtually no end to the themed gifts you can give during the holidays.

You probably wouldn't want to fill a Mason jar with turkey, but on Thanksgiving candy corn is a suitable gift. After all, thanksgiving was all about gift giving, not just stuffing your face until it's completely full! Share that wondrous candy corn! One might not know what to give on a leap year, but it's certainly a rare occasion. Make something up to celebrate this too! Weddings are beautiful occasions, and also a time of gift exchange. The groom could certainly use a couple of cigars to celebrate, and the bride will need a new garter to replace the one she's tossed. On birthdays you've got to take the individual into account, but it should clearly be something that caters to a particular taste. Don't forget what the receiver likes! And remember that above all, it's the thought that counts.

There are other times when people celebrate special events in their lives. High school and university graduation are two big ones. These days computers are a popular gift for high school graduates, but remember, a smart phone may fit within a jar as well. University graduation is an important time too and should be celebrated comparably. After this, a person must go out into the world and transition from being primarily a receiver of Mason jars to a giver of them. This can be a difficult thing to get used to, but with the information here at hand, it should be no problem at all! And how about Bar and Bat Mitzvahs? All the children of the world deserve Mason jar glasses.

CPSIA information can be obtained
at www.ICGtesting.com
Printed in the USA
LVHW031010090821
694847LV00004B/576